The Official Chelsea Football Club Annual 2006

Written by David Clayton

A Grange Publication

© 2005. Published by Grange Communications Ltd., Edinburgh, under licence from Chelsea Football Club. Printed in the EU.

Photographs © Action Images

ISBN 1 902704 91 6

£6.99

Contents

Welcome to the 2006 Official Chelsea Annual!

We hope you enjoy reading about the Blues' stars and re-living some of their amazing achievements of last season as well as looking forward to the prospect of yet more silverware this season.

There are quizzes, player profiles, statistics and puzzles to solve. There are also special features on José Mourinho, John Terry and Frank Lampard and posters of all your favourite players.

So what are you waiting for? Get stuck in, as John Terry would say, and enjoy the CFC Annual 2006!

Captain Fantastic

If anyone could keep the Blue flag flying single-handed, it would be Chelsea skipper John Terry – the original captain fantastic

John Terry entered the world on December 7, 1980. A Barking lad, he would sign for Chelsea as a teenager having turned down Manchester United and gradually rise though the youth teams until October 1998, when aged just 17, he made his debut for the Blues in a League Cup tie against Aston Villa. He played four league games that season and a couple more the following campaign before being loaned to Nottingham Forest for six games during 1999/2000 and they drew three and won three in his time there.

He gained valuable experience while at the City Ground and became a first team regular for Chelsea when Claudio Ranieri took over from Gianluca Vialli as manager. From then on, Terry's star shone brighter than ever and in 2001 he was voted the Player of the Year by Blues fans that recognised the 20 year-old's excellent contribution.

The next season he captained the England Under-21 side and two years later, in June 2003, he made his senior debut for England against Serbia and Montenegro – the first of 17 caps up to the start of the 2005/06 campaign. He played a vital part in England's progress to the last eight of Euro 2004 and when Marcel Desailly left the Bridge last summer, new boss José Mourinho installed Terry as his new captain.

He was inspirational throughout the season, playing 53 games and scoring 8 goals – 4 of them in the Champions League! The first trophy of his captaincy came in the Carling Cup victory over Liverpool and there was no prouder man than John Terry when he lifted the Premiership trophy a few months later. He then received the ultimate tribute from his fellow professionals who voted him 2005 PFA Player of the Year.

An inspirational leader, a terrific defender who can score goals as well as prevent them, his manager José Mourinho claimed he was "the best centre back in the world" – high praise indeed, but thoroughly deserved for a player with Blue blood running through his veins.

9

Mr Motivator

"What I want is to create a football team in my image and in relation to my football philosophy."

The words above were among the first spoken by José Mourinho during his first press conference as Chelsea manager. He told the gathered journalists what his ambitions were and he added that he thought he was "a special one" when it came to management. Twelve months down the line and he had proved just what a special manager he is after steering the Blues to the Premiership title with games to spare, guiding his team to Carling Cup glory and almost taking them to the Champions League final for good measure. And all done in the style Chelsea fans demand, too!

It was an amazing first year in charge at the Bridge for the Portuguese boss and all this comes on the back of his amazing success at Porto, a team he built and won the Champions League with in 2004. Quite simply he is the best manager in Europe and the perfect man to take the Blues to even greater heights.

His style is unique and measured, mixed with superb organisational skills, tactical genius and first-rate man-management ability. He is both the manager and the head coach, overseeing all playing levels within the club. Based predominantly around a solid defence, his midfield is both hard working and inventive and in Damien Duff and Arjen Robben, Chelsea possess two of the most devastating wide men in Europe. He installed a team ethic built around mental strength and inner belief and his first decision was to make John Terry the leader of his team on the pitch.

He is young, confident and focused and hopefully going to manage Chelsea for many years to come. He did in one season what other managers had been trying to do for the previous 49 years by winning the league title - and this is just the beginning. He speaks his mind and isn't afraid to say if he feels his team have suffered an injustice – even if it occasionally lands him in hot water!

All he needs to do now is ensure the trophy cabinet is big enough and order plenty of silver polish for the coming years!

Ever Seen Chelsea Win the League? Actually, Yes....

With what for many clubs would be a whole team's worth of top talent leaving Stamford Bridge during the summer of 2004 and a new manager at the helm, many believed it would take time for the new multi-million pound signings to gel. Among those to leave the Bridge were Jimmy Floyd Hasselbaink, Boudewijn Zenden, Marcel Desailly, Mario Melchiot, Mario Stanic, Jesper Gronkjaer, Winston Bogarde, Neil Sullivan and Emmanuelle Petit. Mikael Forssell and Carlton Cole were loaned out to Birmingham and Aston Villa respectively, for the season. There were also season long loans for Juan Sebastian Veron to Inter Milan and for Hernan Crespo at AC Milan.

José Mourinho arrived to take charge having guided Porto to Champions League glory just weeks earlier and he was determined to bring success immediately and he set about bringing in fresh talent to strengthen a still formidable squad.

Petr Cech, Arjen Robben and Mateja Kezman were early arrivals before Mourinho drafted in two defenders he knew would be excellent additions having both played for him at Porto – Paulo Ferreira and Ricardo Carvalho. Tiago signed from Benfica and Alexey Smertin returned from loan at Portsmouth to start his Chelsea career in earnest. Didier Drogba was also bought from Marseille.

With a rich vein of English talent already at the club in the form of Frank Lampard, Joe Cole, Scott Parker, Wayne Bridge, Glen Johnson and, of course, John Terry, Mourinho now felt he had the strength in-depth for every department of his squad as they set about landing the Blues' first top-flight title since 1955.

Pre-season saw many of the new signings impress during a trip to the USA where Celtic and AS Roma were confidently dispatched but AC Milan triumphed 3-2. The fixture planners could not have come up with a more exciting start to the 2004/05 Premiership campaign by pitting the Blues against Manchester United. It was the supreme test for the new-look Chelsea in a game that Mourinho felt was crucial in shaping their campaign. It took just 15 minutes for the hosts to take the lead, with Eidur Gudjohnsen collecting Drogba's knockdown to score what would be the only goal of the game. It was just the start Mourinho had hoped for and proved his side were resilient against one of our main rivals for the title. The next match at Birmingham, however, could easily have ended in defeat but for fine keeping from Cech and a couple of shots hitting the woodwork. But the true stamp of a quality side was evident when substitute Joe Cole grabbed the only goal of the game, despite having clung on at times.

Joe Cole

Eidur Gudjohnsen

13

The winning run continued at Crystal Palace where Drogba and Tiago scored the goals in a 2-0 win which put the Blues top for the first time but they found themselves 1-0 down at home to Southampton after just 12 seconds thanks to James Beattie's spectacular effort. But the same player put through his own net later in the half and Frank Lampard scored the winner from the spot before half-time. The win meant the Blues had won the first four games of the season in the top division for the first time ever and meant they shared the lead with Arsenal, though the Gunners were top on goal difference.

A 0-0 draw at Aston Villa kept the goals against column clean again and Mourinho later claimed it was the best performance so far by his team. Spurs became the first team to leave the Bridge with a point after another 0-0 draw as goals continued to be hard to come by and their tactics frustrated the manager and supporters. But it was back to winning ways at Middlesbrough where Drogba's strike settled the game in the second half.

The team was unchanged for the third successive game when Liverpool visited for the first game of October. In a tight affair, Cole struck the only goal, flicking home Lampard's low free-kick for yet another 1-0 victory – nobody was going to roll this Chelsea side over with Cech, William Gallas, Claude Makelele, Lampard and skipper Terry all in sparkling form. The next game was away to Manchester City, a team the Blues always seemed to beat in the Premiership, particularly away from the Bridge, but it was to be the only hiccup in a near-perfect season. Nicolas Anelka chased a long through ball with Ferreira on 11 minutes and the pair tangled around the edge of the box. It could and perhaps should have been no more than a free-kick but the referee awarded a penalty and Anelka confidently sent Cech the wrong way for the only goal of the game. Three dropped points allowed Arsenal to move five points ahead at the top of the table with a far superior goal difference but Mourinho was unfazed, believing that the goals would come sooner rather than later. In fact, statistics proved the Blues were the most attacking team in the Premiership so the mechanics were all in place.

Tiago

14

Claude Makelele

The news that leading scorer Drogba would have to be out for seven weeks was tapered by the recovery of Arjen Robben, who, after sustaining a foot injury in pre-season, was raring to show Blues' fans what he could do.

Blackburn Rovers were the team that finally succumbed to a Stamford Bridge thrashing as Chelsea treated the home support to a 4-0 win with three goals from Gudjohnsen (his first professional hat-trick) and another from Damien Duff. The Blues struck four more at West Brom with Gallas, Gudjohnsen, Duff and Lampard on the score sheet in a 4-1 win. Within two games, the goals scored column had doubled giving things a much more balanced look and at last Chelsea sat top of the Premiership again, a position they would remain in for the remainder of the season. It was back to the 1-0 wins with a late winner from Robben deservedly giving the Blues a 1-0 win at Everton.

The league leaders then beat Fulham in the West London derby 4-1 at Craven Cottage which included three stunning goals from Robben, Lampard and Tiago to consolidate the place at the top of the table but a 2-2 draw with Bolton was something of a disappointment, especially after leading 2-0. Beating Charlton 4-0 soon erased that memory and among the scorers at The Valley was John Terry, who opened his Premiership account with two in three minutes

The Blues were really beginning to motor now and had the look of a team that believed it was on the way to the title. There was still much hard work ahead but the momentum was gathering and another 4-0 win, this time at home to Newcastle, emphasised that when Chelsea clicked, they were unstoppable. Goals from Lampard, Drogba, Robben and – at last – Kezman – sealed a fantastic win. With José Mourinho's first manager of the month award in the bag, a superior goal difference to Arsenal and a five point lead at the top, things were looking rosy.

Next up were Arsenal and the biggest test of the new leaders' title credentials to date – the game would not disappoint as it ebbed and flowed with Thierry Henry giving the Gunners an early lead and skipper Terry levelling from a corner. With referee Graham Poll allowing Arsenal to take a quick free kick and re-take the lead as the Blues began to line-up for a wall, it took a clever header from Gudjohnsen to earn a point.

If 1-0 had been an early favourite score-line, 4-0 was becoming equally popular as Norwich became the latest victims of the Blues' formidable attacking prowess in an easy win. Over the Christmas programme the Blues beat Aston Villa 1-0 on Boxing Day, won 2-0 at Portsmouth two days later and secured a 1-0 win at Liverpool on New Year's Day. Maximum points was exactly what Mourinho's boys needed and it was followed by another win without conceding at home to Middlesbrough, thanks to a double strike from Drogba. The gap over second placed Arsenal was now seven points and there was no sign of the 'blip' in form many pundits felt was sure to come along.

Jiri Jarosik was the only signing during the January transfer window; the tall midfielder joined from CSKA Moscow as back-up for Scott Parker who was ruled out of the remaining games with a broken foot. The winning streak continued with a 2-0 victory at Spurs with Lampard scoring both goals and a 3-0 win at the Bridge over Portsmouth further demoralised the Blues' title challengers who wondered how the points gap could possibly be reduced. It was now into double figures with Arsenal losing at Bolton and already it seemed the Blues could not be stopped in their quest for the championship. Another manager of the month award for José was followed by a tough but professional display at Blackburn. The Blues had shown their steel when they needed to most and the only downside of the bruising encounter was the loss of Robben with a fracture in his foot. The team spirit showed in that match was, in many of the players' minds, the final piece of the jigsaw. If the team could withstand such a physical and mental test as that, they had nothing to fear from anyone.

The visit of Manchester City offered Mourinho's boys the chance to avenge their only league defeat of the season but thanks to a miraculous performance by England keeper David James, a resolute City again frustrated the Blues in a 0-0 draw. Another hard-fought win at Everton followed, before the distraction of involvement in three cup competitions had allowed Manchester United to claw back to within five points of the lead going into March. But the Blues had two games in hand as they ran out at Norwich and the 3-1 restored a healthy advantage at the top. Leon McKenzie's goal was the first conceded by Petr Cech in 1024 minutes – a new Premiership record and an amazing achievement by the 22-year-old and the entire defence.

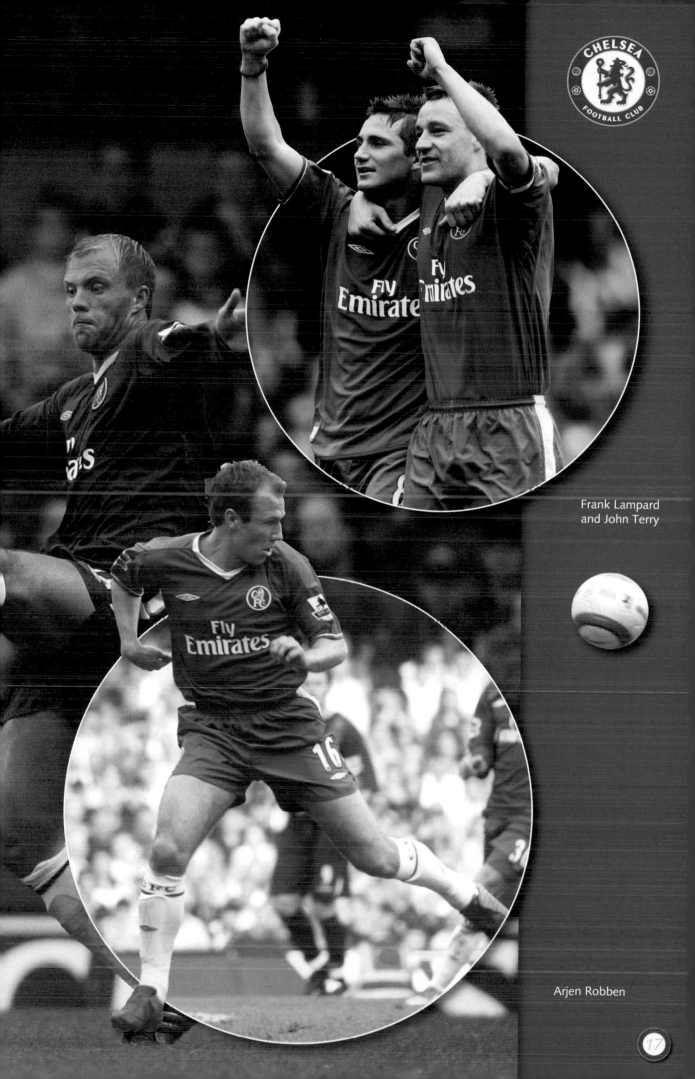

Frank Lampard
and John Terry

Arjen Robben

As the club celebrated its centenary on March 14, a 1-0 win over West Brom a day later proved the perfect birthday present for everyone connected with CFC. A 4-1 win over Crystal Palace followed that and a 3-1 triumph at Southampton gave the Blues a 13-point lead at the top and needing just three more wins to seal the title. It was a fantastic position to be in and one that was fully merited. Birmingham earned a 1-1 draw at the Bridge and Arsenal also took a point with a 0-0 draw a few days later. On the 50th anniversary of the club's only league title, the Blues beat Fulham 3-1 – and the title was once again within touching distance. With four games to go, a win at Bolton would seal the championship. The Boys in Blue would not disappoint.

With thousands of Chelsea fans travelling to the Reebok Stadium, the party atmosphere really began when Lampard opened the scoring with just half-an-hour to go and it was the same player who made it 2-0 late on. Chelsea were champions and deservedly so! The celebrations went on into the early hours and the following days as Blues' fans lapped it up – and why not? They had waited 50 years for this moment. There were more champagne corks popped after Claude Makelele's late goal secured a 1-0 win over Charlton and then the Blues set a new record for Premiership points by beating Manchester United 3-1 at Old Trafford and ended a wonderful season with a 1-1 draw at Newcastle. A fantastic effort by Mourinho's team with much, much more to come.

Frank Lampard

Eidur Gudjohnsen

Joe Cole

2004/05 Season Quiz

Test your knowledge of the Blues' championship-winning season!

1   Name the first player to score against Chelsea last season.

2   Who was the first side to score more than one goal against the Blues?

3   Name the club Alexey Smertin scored his first Chelsea goal against.

4   Which club did Chelsea beat to go top of the Premiership for the first time of the season?

5   True or False? The biggest crowd Chelsea played in front of was 71,622 against Liverpool in the Carling Cup final.

6   Who was the only team not to concede a goal in both Premiership fixtures against the Blues last season?

7   Who did Mateja Kezman score his first Premiership goal against?

8   Who was the only player to play against and for Chelsea last season?

9   Who was the first player to score after coming on as substitute and who was it against?

10 How many consecutive Premiership clean sheets did Petr Cech keep last season and which player finally ended the run?

Answers on page 61

2004/05 Statistics

FINAL LEAGUE TABLE

		Pld	Home					Away					GD	Pts	Top scorer
			W	D	L	F	A	W	D	L	F	A			
1	Chelsea (C)	38	14	5	0	35	6	15	3	1	37	9	57	95	Frank Lampard 13
2	Arsenal	38	13	5	1	54	19	12	3	4	33	17	51	83	Thierry Henry 25
3	Manchester United	38	12	6	1	31	12	10	5	4	27	14	32	77	Wayne Rooney 11
4	Everton	38	12	2	5	24	15	6	5	8	21	31	-1	61	Tim Cahill 11
5	Liverpool	38	12	4	3	31	15	5	3	11	21	26	11	58	Milan Baros 9
6	Bolton Wanderers	38	9	5	5	25	18	7	5	7	24	26	5	58	El-Hadji Diouf 9
7	Middlesbrough	38	9	6	4	29	19	5	7	7	24	27	7	55	Jimmy Floyd Hasselbaink 13
8	Manchester City	38	8	6	5	24	14	5	7	7	23	25	8	52	Shaun Wright-Phillips 10
9	Tottenham Hotspur	38	9	5	5	36	22	5	5	9	11	19	6	52	Jermain Defoe 13
10	Aston Villa	38	8	6	5	26	17	4	5	10	19	35	-7	47	Nolberto Solano 8
11	Charlton Athletic	38	8	4	7	29	29	4	6	9	13	29	-16	46	Shaun Bartlett 6
12	Birmingham City	38	8	6	5	24	15	3	6	10	16	31	-6	45	Emile Heskey 10
13	Fulham	38	8	4	7	29	26	4	4	11	23	34	-8	44	Andy Cole 12
14	Newcastle United	38	7	7	5	25	25	3	7	9	22	32	-10	44	Alan Shearer 7
15	Blackburn Rovers	38	5	8	6	21	22	4	7	8	11	21	-11	42	Paul Dickov 9
16	Portsmouth	38	8	4	7	30	26	2	5	12	13	33	-16	39	Yakubu Ayegbeni 13
17	West Bromwich Albion	38	5	8	6	17	24	1	8	10	19	37	-25	34	Robert Earnshaw 11
18	Crystal Palace (R)	38	6	5	8	21	19	1	7	11	20	43	-21	33	Andrew Johnson 21
19	Norwich City (R)	38	7	5	7	29	32	0	7	12	13	45	-35	33	Damien Francis 7
20	Southampton (R)	38	5	9	5	30	30	1	5	13	15	36	-21	32	Peter Crouch 12

Petr Cech

Glen Johnson

	Age	Appearances				Goals				Chelsea career	
		FAPL	FAC	UCL	LC	FAPL	FAC	UCL	LC	Apps	Goals
Celestine **Babayaro**	26	3+1			1					177+20	8
Wayne **Bridge**	24	12+3	2	4	4					68+5	3
Ricardo **Carvalho**	27	22+3	1	10	3	1				36+3	1
Petr **Cech**	23	35		11	2	24 cs		4 cs		48	28 cs
Joe **Cole**	23	19+9	3	8+1	4+2	8		1		59+37	12
Carlo **Cudicini**	31	3	3	1	4		1 cs	1 cs	3 cs	167+3	74 cs
Didier **Drogba**	27	18+8	1+1	8+1	3+1	10		5	1	30+11	16
Damien **Duff**	26	28+2	1+1	8+2	5+1	6		2	2	68+17	16
Paulo **Ferreira**	26	29	0+1	6+1	5					40+2	0
Mikael **Forssell**	24	0+1		0+1						12+41	12
William **Gallas**	27	28	1	12	5	2				169+11	9
Geremi	26	6+7	2	1+3	1					40+19	1
Anthony **Grant**	18	0+1								0+1	0
Eidur **Gudjohnsen**	26	30+7	2+1	9+2	1+5	12(1p)	1	2	1	152+74	75 (5p)
Robert **Huth**	20	6+4	1	1+3		1				21+20	2
Jiri **Jarosik**	27	3+11	2+1		1+2					6+14	0
Glen **Johnson**	20	13+4	3	4+2	2+1					51+10	4
Mateja **Kezman**	26	6+19	3	3+6	2+2	4(1p)	1		2	14+27	7 (1p)
Frank **Lampard**	27	38	0+2	12	3+3	13(3p)		4	2	204+13	49 (5p)
Claude **Makelele**	32	36		10	4	1				91+5	1
Nuno **Morais**	21	0+2	1	0+1						1+3	0
Adrian **Mutu**	26	0+2								30+8	10
Filipe **Oliveira**	21	0+1								0+8	0
Scott **Parker**	24	1+3		3+1	3					19+9	1
Lenny **Pidgeley**	21	0+1								0+1	1 cs
Arjen **Robben**	21	14+4	0+2	2+3	3+1	7		1	1	19+10	9
Alexey **Smertin**	30	11+5	3	4+1	1			1		19+6	1
John **Terry**	24	36	1	11	5	3	1	4		204+18	23
Tiago	24	21+13	2	4+7	4	4				31+20	4
Steven **Watt**	20	0+1	1							1+1	0

Opponents' own goals: 4

Name Game Quiz

Work out the name of these Chelsea players by re-arranging the words below...

1. CUICID LION CAR   _ _ _ _ _ _   _ _ _ _ _ _ _ _

2. JOB NEAR R BEN   _ _ _ _ _ _   _ _ _ _ _ _

3. DREAD BIO GRID   _ _ _ _ _ _ _   _ _ _ _ _ _

4. I ALL SWIG A MALL   _ _ _ _ _ _ _   _ _ _ _ _ _

5. LAME DUCK ALE EEL   _ _ _ _ _ _   _ _ _ _ _ _ _ _

6. HARD COIL ROAR VAC   _ _ _ _ _ _ _ _   _ _ _ _ _ _ _ _ _

7. U FIND FAMED   _ _ _ _ _ _   _ _ _ _ _

8. HURT BOTHER   _ _ _ _ _ _   _ _ _ _ _

9. DANK LARK FARM   _ _ _ _ _ _   _ _ _ _ _ _ _

10. I GOAT   _ _ _ _ _ _

Check your answers on page 61

HANDS UP

WHO WANTS TO BE A TRUE BLUE?

If you're into Chelsea, we're looking for fresh legs to join the Junior True Blue membership scheme.

For just £15, it gives you all this:

- Priority ticket allocation for home matches
- An exclusive members' kit bag packed with loads of goodies
- Quarterly Junior Blues magazine
- Birthday and Christmas cards from the team
- Members' only website
- TeamCard
- Fan days

...and much more besides!

It couldn't be easier to apply. You and your parents or your guardian can do it now online. Or you can call us today for an application form.

Go on – be part of a winning team!

WWW.CHELSEAFC.COM
0870 300 1212
Lines are open Mon-Fri 9am-5pm

TRUE BLUE

OFFICIAL CHELSEA MEMBERSHIP

Word Search

Figure out what the clues represent. Then find the words in the grid.
Words can go horizontally, vertically and diagonally in all eight directions.

```
M  J  K  D  Z  E  I  D  U  R  N  B
D  R  N  G  N  I  L  R  A  C  G  H
C  L  E  G  T  K  T  O  D  R  T  V
X  E  P  K  B  M  O  F  W  T  G  V
Z  S  N  L  R  G  M  M  B  M  J  H
C  D  R  T  A  A  R  A  C  O  L  E
O  R  R  I  E  A  P  T  K  K  F  H
B  O  T  O  N  N  L  S  O  H  Z  X
H  C  T  I  M  Z  A  T  T  O  T  K
A  E  E  Q  H  A  R  R  L  J  H  H
M  R  B  L  K  O  N  A  Y  J  R  T
I  L  O  O  P  R  E  V  I  L  K  Q
```

CLUES

Name of our mascot

Carlton who spent time at Aston Villa

Name of new training facility

Claudio, the last Italian manager

Team the Blues played 5 times in 04/05

Chelsea broke plenty of these last season

Midfielder who uses only one name

José's former club

In 2005, the club celebrated its...............

Former crowd idol Gianfranco

First cup won under José

Scott, who left for Newcastle

Mr Abramovich's first name

Icelandic forward's first name

Denied by a Flag!

– The Story of the Blues' 2004/05 Champions League Adventure

So near and yet so far – the Blues could well have been enjoying the title of European champions had a controversial decision not gone against them in the semi-final, but there was a lot of excitement, thrills and spills in the previous rounds as Mourinho's boys took on – and beat – many of Europe's top sides. In many ways, the Champions League performances were different to the disciplined and focused displays in the Premiership. Of course, the desire to win is the same every time Mourinho sends out his team, but there was an electrical charge running through the Bridge for Champions League nights and the Blues responded with several remarkable victories that would take them to within a whisker of the final. This is how each round unfurled...

Group Stages:

The Blues were drawn in Group H - the same group as José Mourinho's former club Porto, the champions of Europe! The drama had already begun without a ball being kicked! CSKA Moscow and Paris St Germain completed what looked like a tricky group.

PSG 3-0 (a) – 14/9/04

Paris had failed to win a game of any kind prior to this match and that wasn't going to change for the visit of the Blues, who had Didier Drogba, who used to play for PSG's deadly rivals Marseille, leading the line. But it was John Terry who opened the scoring, heading home a Frank Lampard corner. Drogba made it 2-0 on the stroke of half-time – and as the ball nestled in the net he ran over to the Paris fans, who had booed him all night, to mock them and point to his name on the back of his shirt. And it was Drogba who made it 3-0 with a lovely free kick that he celebrated again in front of the home fans. The Blues were off and running!

Porto 3-1 (h) – 29/9/04

The visit of Porto was a special evening for José Mourinho and both sets of supporters. Alexey Smertin volleyed home the opening goal in the first half and Drogba's clever header made it 2-0 before Benni McCarthy pulled one back. But cometh the hour, cometh the man and from Lampard's free kick Terry dived in to head a wonderful third goal to seal the game and leave the Blues two points clear at the top of Group H.

CSKA 2-0 (h) – 20/10/04

John Terry became joint top scorer in European competition for the Blues with his third headed goal in succession, this time against CSKA and again it was from a Lampard cross. Two magnificent saves from Petr Cech kept the Russians out before Gudjohnsen's header sealed the win.

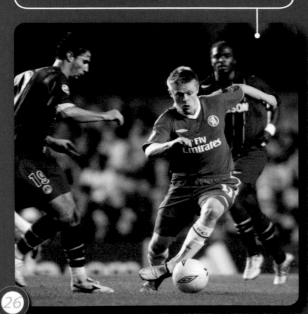

CSKA 1-0 (a) – 2/11/04

This was a disciplined performance by the Blues who maintained their 100% record so far in Moscow. It was the club's first competitive game in Russia and it was also the first time Arjen Robben and Damien Duff had started in the side at the same time. Playing all in white, the winner came from a delightful move involving Duff and Robben, with the flying Dutch winger finishing the move in style. It was a goal worthy of winning any game and thanks to CSKA missing a penalty, that's exactly what it did!

PSG 0-0 (h) – 24/11/05

Not a wonderful game as the Blues took the chance to rotate the squad having already qualified for the next stage. PSG had the better chances but a draw was a fair result.

Knock-out Stages:

Barcelona 1-2 (a) leg 1, 23/2/05

Eleven weeks had passed since the defeat to Porto but from the minute the Blues were paired with Barcelona for the right to progress to the last eight, the whole of Europe had been eagerly awaiting this clash. Both teams were among the favourites to win the competition and this would be the ultimate test for the Blues - but one Mourinho was delighted to have. He wanted to test his side against the best and he felt Barcelona were possibly the best opposition they could face at that point. A heavy loss at the Nou Camp and the Blues would be almost certainly out but the dramatic events of this match would mean the tie would go back to West London finely balanced. In the early stages, the Blues were happy to soak up the pressure and threaten on the break and it was a lightening quick move that lead to the opening goal. Lampard's 40-yard pass sent Duff clear and his cross was turned in by Belletti for an own goal. Shortly after, Drogba raced clear but put his shot wide of the post and many Blues wondered if it wouldn't prove a costly miss by the Frenchman. Shortly after the break Drogba's challenge on the Barca keeper was harshly deemed a foul and he was shown a second yellow card and sent off – it was going to be uphill from there on! Gradually, the home team wore down the Blues' defence with constant waves of attacks and goals from Lopez and Eto'o swung the tie Barca's way and they had several chances to kill the Blues off but the score remained 2-1.

Porto 1-2 (a) – 7/12/05

It was always going to be an emotional return for José Mourinho who just a year earlier had been masterminding Porto's path to Champions League glory. Duff's goal suggested it might be a triumphant return to Portugal for the manager but goals from Diego and McCarthy enabled Porto to progress to the next round with a 2-1 win.

Barcelona 4-2 (h) leg 2, 8/3/05

This match will live long in the memory of those who witnessed it as the Blues went for the kill from the very first minute, which was all they could do if they wanted to progress. It was a game that had everything – goals, controversy and high drama as the tie swung one way and then the other. The Blues couldn't have wished for a better start with a breakaway goal finished by Gudjohnsen after just seven minutes. Ten minutes later, Lampard finished from close range after Joe Cole's shot had been saved and with less than 20 minutes on the clock, Duff raced away to make it 3-0, sending the Bridge into raptures. Barca had been defensively awful but they still had the talent to save themselves and when Ferreira handled in the box, Ronaldinho scored from the spot to put a different complexion on the night. If Barca could find another goal, it would be they who were going through, not Chelsea. Step forward that man Ronaldinho again to score a stunning individual goal from the edge of the box. Cole then hit the post before the referee blew for half-time – yes – all that happened in the first 45!! It gave everyone a chance to get their breath back, too! Barca hit the post and came close again before (who else?) John Terry popped up to head what proved to be a late winner. A fantastic game between two fantastic teams and a night nobody will forget in a hurry.

Quarter-final
Bayern Munich 4-2 (h) leg 1, 6/4/05

With Mourinho banned from the dressing room and touchline for his views on referee Anders Frisk in the previous round, the Blues faced the mighty Bayern Munich knowing they had to take some kind of advantage to Germany. Again, it proved to be a memorable night. It took just four minutes for the Blues to score with Cole's deflected shot fooling the Bayern keeper and rolling into the net. That was the score at the break and it was the Germans who scored next to level the tie but Lampard restored the lead with a well-taken drive from the edge of the box. His second of the game put Chelsea in control of the match. Drogba made it 4-1 before a late penalty was converted in injury time to add a new edge to the second leg.

Bayern Munich 2-3 (a) leg 2, 12/4/05

Yet another deflected goal virtually sealed this tie as Lampard's long-range effort found the net to give the Blues a 5-2 aggregate lead. Both teams had chances to score before Bayern equalised in the second half and then began to apply the pressure before Drogba scored a brilliant header to seal the victory. Two late goals from Bayern gave them a 3-2 win but it was too little, too late.

Liverpool 0-0 (h) leg 1, 27/4/05

The battle for a place in the final meant that at least one English side would play in Istanbul and most expected Chelsea to be that team. But this game would prove a frustrating night for the Blues as chance after chance went begging. Drogba, Lampard and Terry had opportunities they uncharacteristically missed and the teams went back to Anfield level.

Liverpool 0-1 (a) leg 2, 3/5/05

Having just been crowned Premiership champions, it was back to business for Chelsea as they travelled to Merseyside for a fifth meeting of the season with Liverpool. With three wins and a draw in the previous meetings, hopes were high of further success but it was Liverpool who scored the only goal of the game in the most dramatic circumstances. With just three minutes gone, Luis Garcia followed up Baros' shot to hook the ball goalwards. William Gallas seemed to clear the ball off the line but the referee's assistant flagged to indicate a goal. Technology would later indicate the ball did not cross the line but none of that mattered because the officials gave the goal. The Blues fought hard for an equaliser and Gudjohnsen had a good chance deep into injury time but volleyed inches wide. José Mourinho later claimed the best team lost and few disagreed with that view. Liverpool would go on to win the Champions League final while Mourinho began planning for next year's campaign.

CHAMPIONS
CHELSEA FOOTBALL CLUB
2004 ~ 2005

CHELSEA FOOTBALL CLUB

KJW 296W

30

THE Stadium TOUR >>>>

AND MUSEUM

VISIT THE HOME OF THE CHAMPIONS

Do not miss this once in a lifetime opportunity to visit the brand new museum and take the fantastic behind the scenes tour of Stamford Bridge, home of the Barclays Premiership Champions 2005!

Our superb guided tours take you into parts of the stadium you thought you'd never see! The press room, the interview rooms, the Managers' Dugouts and, best of all, the magnificent Chelsea home dressing room.

Come and see where our record breaking squad prepare for games, feel the tension as you line-up in the Players' Tunnel and take the seat of our illustrious manager José Mourinho where he gives his all important press conference.

This tour is a must for Chelsea fans of all ages and is a perfect birthday or Christmas present, so call and book your tickets now!

TOURS BOOKING LINE: 0870 603 0005

FOR ENQUIRIES AND CFC CHILDRENS BIRTHDAY PARTIES, CALL 0207 957 8278

tour bookings subject to availability

Cech Mate!

Is Petr Cech the best goalkeeper in the world? The statistics suggest he is...

Petr Cech began his rise to the top in world football with his hometown club Viktoria Plzen. He was born in the Czech Republic on May 20, 1982 and 17 years later, after never playing a senior game for Plzen, he made his debut for his new club Chmel Blsany. That match was his only game of the 1999/2000 season but the following year the strapping 18 year-old played 26 times for Chmel and it was during this time he was spotted by one of the top Czech clubs, Sparta Prague.

Petr was signed by Sparta with the future in mind – but four games into the 2001/02 campaign, he took over as No.1 and played 26 times in the league. He also set a new Czech record by going 928 minutes without conceding a goal – over 10 matches! Yet again he had attracted the attention of another side and surprisingly signed for French club Rennes who were certainly not one of the leading clubs in France.

Cech played 37 times in his first year, helping Rennes stay in the top division and the following season he was inspirational in helping them finish fourth – but by this point, a deal had been struck between the Blues and Rennes that Cech would be a Chelsea player for the 2004/05 season!

He made his Premiership debut against Manchester United and, as a sign of things to come, kept a clean sheet during a 1-0 win. His form throughout Chelsea's championship-winning year was exceptional with many breathtaking saves along the way and several instinctive stops that defied belief.

Thierry Henry's quick free kick in the 2-2 draw with Arsenal saw Cech unfairly criticised by some who felt he should have been ready for the unexpected. But those same people were forced to eat their words as Cech then kept 11 consecutive clean sheets in the Premiership, smashing the record held by Peter Schmeichel and his total of 1024 without conceding will take some beating.

By the end of the season, he'd also broken the Premiership record for most clean sheets in a season and was awarded the Golden Glove for his achievements. He was voted in the PFA's Premiership team of the season and during last summer he was awarded the Golden Ball for being the Czech Republic's 2005 player of the season – the first goalkeeper to ever win the award.

All in all, it's been quite a season for Petr Cech who is still only 23 years-old and surely already the best goalkeeper in the world...

Chelsea Centenary

One Hundred Not Out!

Despite Chelsea Football Club being founded on March 14, 1905, the club decided, after much debate, to make the 2005/06 season our Centenary Year rather than the calendar year of 2005 itself.

This momentous football year will be celebrated with numerous exciting events with the people who matter most – the supporters – participating fully during the season.

The Blues' first match was on September 2, 1905 at Stockport County. Since this was the first time the club was officially actually in action on the pitch, we decided that this season merited Centenary status rather than 2005 alone.

An overall programme of events through 2005 and the 2005/6 season has already been drawn up with football as the centre piece. But people around the world recognize that the name Chelsea goes beyond football. It is synonymous with fashion, music and art and is part of the social history of not just our immediate home in Hammersmith and Fulham, but of London as a whole.

The celebrations will also reflect this so there will be plenty for people of all ages and tastes to participate in and we want you to celebrate our 100th birthday because without you, there'd be no party!

This is just the beginning of what should be a fantastic time for Chelsea Football Club and we will continue to keep you informed of developments.

Now, who gets to cut the cake...?

Magic Lamps!

With the family pedigree Frank Lampard has, he was always destined to enjoy a career at the very top of the English game from the moment he first kicked a ball around the garden as a toddler. His father Frank enjoyed two FA Cup final victories with West Ham during a long distinguished career for the East London side, while uncle Harry Redknapp also played for the Hammers before becoming a successful manager and cousin Jamie Redknapp went on to play for Liverpool and Spurs.

A huge crowd favourite at Upton Park, Lampard Jr was snapped up by Chelsea on June 14, 2001 after he became unsettled following his father's exit from the club. This was followed by the surprise exit of Uncle Harry and the sale of his close friend Rio Ferdinand to Leeds. That meant the young England star no longer had anything to tie him to the Hammers and when he arrived at Stamford Bridge he was regarded as one of the best young talents in the country.

He enjoyed two solid seasons in 2001/02 and 2002/03, helping the Blues to gain Champions League football and rarely missed a game. His eye for goal, range of passing and ability to provide pinpoint crosses for others to profit from won him more England caps and during 2004/05 his influence on the Blues grew to indispensable proportions.

Alongside his good friend John Terry, the pair form the English heart of José Mourinho's multi-national side and the new boss was quick to make 'Lamps' his vice captain during his first few weeks at the club.

Last season he surpassed all his previous achievements, scoring an amazing 20 goals from midfield and driving the Blues on to their first league title in 50 years. How fitting, then, that it should be Lampard that scored the goals that sealed the title at Bolton after such a wonderful season.

And to cap things off for the 27 year-old, he picked up the much-coveted English Football Writers player of the year award for 2005 – a prize voted by the journalists who give praise out sparingly. This after being voted runner-up for the second year in succession in the PFA Player of the Year voting and he becomes only the second English player in more than a decade to win the Football Writers' prize.

Crossword

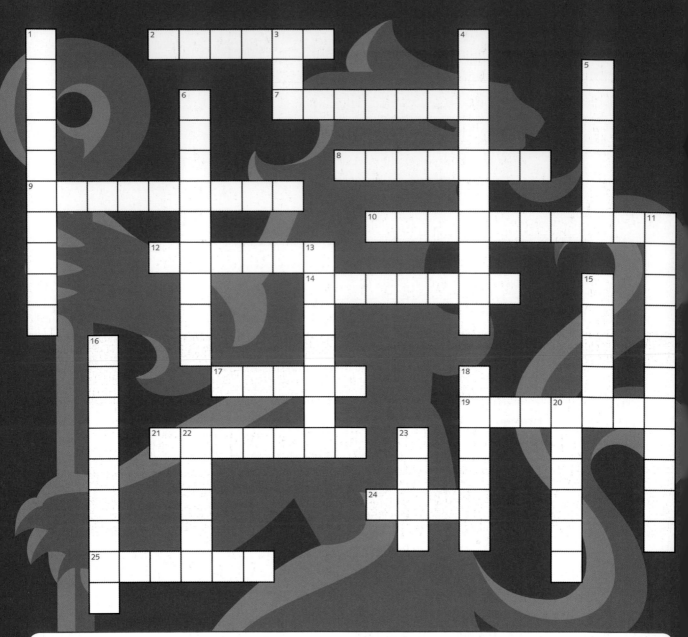

ACROSS

2 Argentinean who played all last season at AC Milan (6)

7 Frank, who cost £5million from Spurs (7)

8 Joe, Glen and Frank signed from this club (4,3)

9 Team never to have beaten the Blues in the Premiership (9)

10 Traditional nickname for the Blues (10)

12 Club Petr Cech joined Chelsea from (6)

14 Reserve team coach Mick (7)

17 Number of years since previous championship win (5)

19 Steven Gerrard scored one of these for us in the Carling Cup (3,4)

21 Stamford Bridge stand (4,3)

24 We'll keep the _____ flag flying high (4)

25 "Blue is the _____" (6)

DOWN

1 Powerhouse German defender (6,4)

3 John Terry won the ___ Award in 2005 (3)

4 The Blues lost their only Premiership game of 04/05 in this city (10)

5 Amount of points the Blues won the title by (6)

6 Captain fantastic! (4,5)

11 Assistant to José (5,6)

13 Alexey, who spent time at Portsmouth (7)

15 Silvino, who coaches the Blues' goalkeepers (5)

16 Chelsea FC PLC Chairman (5,4)

18 Surname of Batman's partner? (6)

20 French international William (6)

22 Asier del _____ who signed from Athletic Bilbao (5)

23 Joe and Carlton's shared surname (4)

Spot the ball!

Look carefully at the picture below and use all of
your skill to work out where the ball might be!

Who are they?

A

B

C

D

E

F

Answers on page 61

Carling Cup Winners!

Carling Cup Winners!

The first trophy of the season for the Blues arrived back in February and was, many hoped, the first of four Chelsea were chasing at home and abroad. But it wasn't an easy passage to Cardiff with local derbies and clashes with top Premiership rivals along the way. This was a trophy, however, that José Mourinho was determined to win and his players responded magnificently. First up was West Ham at Stamford Bridge and the tie certainly caught the imagination of both sets of fans with a full-house watching the Blues edge out the Hammers with a goal from Mateja Kezman – his first for the club. Frank Lampard missed a penalty and Anton Ferdinand hit the bar for the visitors, but the score remained 1-0. Next it was the long journey north to face Newcastle United where substitutes Eidur Gudjohnsen and Arjen Robben eased the Blues into the last eight of the League Cup for the fourth year running.

Fulham at Craven Cottage would prove another tough match and they were keen to avenge a 4-1 league defeat they suffered at the hands of the Blues just a few weeks earlier. Damien Duff gave Chelsea the lead with a deflected shot but Brian McBride equalised and the game seemed to be heading for extra time. But with talent like Lampard to bring off the bench, any game is winnable and with moments remaining, his powerful shot proved too much for the keeper and the Blues were in the last four where they would face Manchester United over two legs. A full-house at the Bridge saw United earn a 0-0 draw despite numerous chances for the home team but justice was done in the return tie when goals from Lampard and Duff were enough to see off United 2-1 and book a place in the final against Liverpool in the final.

40

With 71,622 crammed into the Millennium Stadium the Blues fans created a wall of noise for Mourinho's side but Liverpool struck within a minute of the kick-off and it was a lead they held until Steven Gerrard headed past his own keeper on 79 minutes to send the game into extra time. With José Mourinho banished from the touchline for what was perceived as telling the Liverpool fans to be silent, the Blues raced ahead thanks to a Didier Drogba header and then Kezman stabbed home from close range to render Nunez's late goal for the Reds merely academic. The Blues had won 3-2 and collected their first trophy under José Mourinho and it was nothing less than they deserved.

Where in the World?

Have a look at our world map below to see where the Chelsea stars were born around the world

Eidur Gudjohnsen
Reykjavik, Iceland
(September 15, 1978)

Damien Duff
Ballyboden, Ireland
(March 2, 1979)

William Gallas
Asnieres-sur-Seine, France
(August 17, 1977)

Ricardo Carvalho
Amarante, Portugal
(May 18, 1978)

Paulo Ferreira
Cascais, Portugal
(January 18, 1979)

Asier del Horno
Barakaldo, Spain
(January 19,1981)

Carlo Cudicini
Milan, Italy
(September 6, 1973)

Didier Drogba
Abidjan, Ivory Coast
(March 11,1978)

Frank Lampard
Romford, England
(June 21, 1978)

Shaun Wright Phillips
London, England
(October 25, 1981)

Arjen Robben
Bedum, Netherlands
(January 23, 1984)

Robert Huth
Berlin, Germany
(August 18, 1984)

Petr Cech
Plzen, Czech Republic
(May 20 1982)

Jiri Jarosik
Usti Nad Labem, Czech
Rep (October 27, 1977)

Claude Makelele
Kinsasha, Democratic
Republic of Congo
(February 18, 1973)

Ndjitap Geremi
Bafoussan, Cameroon
(December 20, 1978)

There were so many quality goals last season that choosing a top 10 was always going to be hard – see if you agree with our selections that feature no less than FIVE efforts from one player in particular…

1 - Arjen Robben v CSKA Moscow 2/11/04

Arjen Robben's first goal for the Blues came in Moscow and proved to be the only goal of the game – but what a goal! Cech found the head of Gudjohnsen with a long clearance and he flicked it on to Robben who controlled the ball and instantly played it though to Duff. Duff laid a beautiful back-heel back into Robben's path and he side-stepped one defender with embarrassing ease and then poked it past the keeper. Genius!

2 - Frank Lampard v Bayern Munich 6/4/05

With the Blues desperate for another goal against Bayern Munich, the ball fell to Makelele on the right-hand edge of the box. He saw Lampard free at the far post and chipped the ball across. Lamps chested the ball up, pirouetted and then volleyed the ball past the Munich keeper for a stunning finish.

3 - Arjen Robben v Fulham 13/11/04

Picking up a Fulham clearance 30 yards out, the flying Dutch winger shaped to shoot and left two defenders sprawling on the floor as he danced around them. He then cut inside another two defenders before poking the ball home for another world class goal.

4 - Eidur Gudjohnsen v Southampton 2/4/05

Maybe individually not the most stunning goal, but as a team effort, absolutely superb. It began with Makelele playing it to Gudjohnsen who played a one-two with Lampard before touching off to Drogba. Gudjohnsen continued his run and was fed the ball back by Drogba and finished the move by planting the ball home with a low shot.

5 - Frank Lampard v Bolton 30/4/05

This, well taken goal though it was, was in fact one of Lamps' less spectacular efforts – but seeing it was the goal that clinched the league title after a 50 year wait, it will always be a special goal for the Blues' fans. With a clear run on goal from the halfway line, you just knew he was going to score and when he rounded the home keeper to slot the ball home, the celebrations really began.

6 - Tiago v Manchester United 10/5/05

With nothing much on from 30-yards out, Tiago let fly with a right-foot rocket that left Roy Carroll no more than an admiring bystander – what a strike!

7 - Joe Cole v Norwich 5/3/05

The young England man slipped away from his marker 25 yards out before rifling a left foot bullet past Robert Green for the opening goal of the game at Carrow Road which the Blues eventually won 3-1.

8 - Frank Lampard v Crystal Palace 19/3/05

From his trademark patch, 25 yards out, Lampard picked the ball up in space, nudged it forward and then cracked a superb shot that swerved into the right hand corner.

9 - Frank Lampard v Fulham 13/11/04

With the scores level at 0-0, Lampard ran on to a short pass free-kick routine to hammer a right foot howitzer past Mark Crossley from 30 yards out. A real cracker from the England midfielder and yet another goal against the Cottagers.

10 - Frank Lampard v Norwich City 18/12/04

Arjen Robben's run and pass inside to Lampard left the Blues' No.8 with a clear sight of goal from 25 yards. He took one look up before planting a screamer into the top right-hand corner of the net.

JOSE
MOURINHO
FOR
PRIME MINISTER

Spot the Differences

Study the two pictures below and try to spot the
12 differences between them
(we've given you a start with the first difference)

Player Profiles

Petr Cech

Commanding, agile and already a legend at the Bridge, Petr Cech was one of José Mourinho's first signings and undoubtedly one of the best and most influential. He broke all club records for clean sheets last season and set new Premiership records in the process. A giant presence in every sense of the word, when it comes to the last line of defence, Cech is among the best in the world.

Carlo Cudicini

Carlo is one of the longest serving players at the Bridge these days and only the likes of Terry, Lampard and Gallas can boast more appearances for the Blues in the current squad. Though largely second choice to Cech, Mourinho has great faith in his back-up keeper and only suspension robbed the Italian of a place in the Carling Cup final last season. A popular and dependable member of the squad.

Lenny Pidgeley

Lenny Pidgeley is the Blues' third choice goalkeeper at present but at the age of 21, he has plenty of time to rise in the ranks. So confident in his ability was the new coaching team that they felt comfortable enough to allow the likes of Neil Sullivan, Marco Ambrosio and Jurgen Macho move on. He made his first team debut towards the end of last season; coming on as substitute for Cudicini and making a good save within seconds of arriving.

Glen Johnson

Glen Johnson has shown enough in the past two seasons to suggest he will be one of the top English defenders for many years to come. He'll only be 21 this season and played more than half the games last season, including some fine displays in the Champions League. Has more to his game than just defending and has shown the ability to dribble with the best of them on occasion!

John Terry

What can be said of the Blues' skipper that hasn't already been said this season? Arguably the most coveted English defender at the moment, Terry is a man-mountain in defence and a constant threat to the opposition from set-pieces. Scores almost all his goals with his head and was joint-second top scorer in the Champions League last season for the Blues with four goals. He also won the PFA Player of the Year award for his efforts during 2004/05 and it would be hard to imagine a Chelsea team without him. He will be certain to travel with England to Germany for the 2006 World Cup.

Robert Huth

Having joined the Blues aged 16, the powerful German is now beginning to show what a tremendous addition he can be to the Chelsea squad. Aged just 21, Huth stepped in on several occasions last season and played in both legs against Bayern Munich in the Champions League. Will continue to improve with more games under his belt.

Tiago

Portuguese midfielder Tiago joined from Benfica last season and played some part in the majority of Chelsea matches last season and has shown flair in attack and an ability to defend when needed. Will have benefited from a full season with the Blues and is capable of the odd spectacular goal, such as his fine strike against Manchester United last May

Claude Makelele

One of the Blues' unsung heroes, Claude Makelele sits in front of the defence mopping up, breaking up and generally frustrating the opposition's attacks. The former Real Madrid man's effectiveness was greater than ever last season and he played almost every game of the 2004/5 campaign. He had still not scored when Charlton arrived for the last match of the season and when a last-minute penalty was awarded, it was Makelele who stepped up to take it. With 41,000 fans willing him to beak his duck, his penalty was saved but he was first to the rebound and his goal drought finally ended.

Ricardo Carvalho

When José Mourinho decided he needed a central defender, he turned to a player who had served him well at Porto and signed Portuguese international Ricardo Carvalho. The talented centre-half is dominant both in the air and on the ground and was awarded the UEFA 2004 European Football Award for Best Defender. He was outstanding in his first season in the Blues' defence, but a broken toe forced him out for two months.

Frank Lampard

Few would argue that 'Lamps' is the best English midfielder around at the moment. With seemingly an inexhaustible supply of energy, Lampard bagged an incredible 20 goals from midfield last year and provided countless free-kicks, passes and corners for others to benefit from. Like John Terry, Lampard is the essence of the Chelsea team and one of the first names on José Mourinho's team sheet each week. Priceless and irreplaceable, Lamps is pure class.

Joe Cole

Since the arrival of Mourinho, Joe Cole has continued to improve and is now playing the best football of his career. Words of wisdom from the manager steered him into becoming a better team player and the results of the 'new' Joe Cole were there for all to see last season. A hugely popular player, he has now made it difficult for the boss to leave him out and a series of top-notch displays made him perhaps the Blues' most improved player of 2004/5.

Jiri Jarosik

Signed during the 2005 January transfer window, Jiri Jarosik's performance for CSKA against the Blues in Moscow convinced José Mourinho to sign the tall midfielder as a replacement for the then injured Scott Parker. The 6' 4" Czech can play as an attacking midfielder or a much deeper role. Will have benefited from at least four months worth of Premiership experience.

William Gallas

A defensive rock, William Gallas is a manager's dream, slotting in wherever he's asked and being effective in each role he undertakes. Though he prefers central defence, he filled in admirably for the injured Wayne Bridge for much of last season and never let his team-mates down. He played every Champions League game during the Blues' run to the semi-finals and was one of only two players to achieve the feat. Will challenge Ricardo Carvalho strongly again next season for the spot alongside John Terry.

Geremi

The versatile Cameroon star featured only occasionally during his second season at the Bridge and the fact that he can play many roles meant that there wasn't one specifically for him in Mourinho's team. But the former Real Madrid star, signed two years ago, has vowed to fight for a place and remain a Chelsea player – an attitude that has impressed the manager.

Didier Drogba

The former Marseille striker didn't have quite the season he would have liked last year with a mixture of injury and adapting to the pace of the Premiership affecting his form. He still showed signs of his explosive talent, particularly in the Champions League where he ended top scorer with five goals in six starts and scored several crucial goals in other competitions. One of the best headers in the Premiership, Drogba should be among the top scorers in the division this season.

Arjen Robben

Arjen Robben was an unknown quantity for many Premiership defenders when he finally made his debut three months into the season, having sat out the first few months with injury. When he found his stride, he was among the most talked about players in the Premiership and mixed devastating pace with fantastic individual skill to great effect. Only 21, he played in less than half of the Blues games last year and will be raring to go this season. Never scores anything but spectacular goals and when he and Damien Duff are in full flight, it's a joy to watch.

Wayne Bridge

Desperately unlucky to break his ankle at Newcastle having played his part in the Blues' quest for four trophies up to that point, the England left-back will be fit and ready for the new campaign but will have to challenge Asier del Horno and William Gallas to become a first team regular again.

Paulo Ferreira

Another former Mourinho employee, Paulo Ferreira joined Chelsea in the summer of 2004 from Porto, with the fee creating a new British record for a full-back. Though he can supplement attacks with his excellent crosses, he is yet to score in his professional career, but he has stopped many being scored and is the club's regular right-back.

Upcoming Youngsters

Filipe Oliveira

A rarity – a Portuguese import not signed by José Mourinho! Yet Filipe Oliveira signed for the Blues from Porto but this was just before José arrived to work his magic. A versatile forward who can play on either flank or as a forward, the 21 year-old will be hoping to make an impression this season.

Anthony Grant

An England youth international, Anthony Grant has progressed well in the reserves last season and at just 18 years old, he has plenty of time to impress. He's been with the Blues since he was nine and the versatile youngster played much of last year at right back. Maybe seen around the first team fringes this year.

Nuno Morais

There has been little seen of Nuno Morais so far, the lowest profile Portuguese player to arrive at the club. Clearly bought with the future in mind, Nuno can play comfortably in defence or as a deep midfielder and more may be seen of the Portuguese U-21 star during the 2005/6 campaign.

Steven Watt

Former Scottish youth captain Steven Watt is highly regarded at Chelsea and made his debut in the FA Cup tie against Scunthorpe last January. A strong central defender, who will have benefited from training alongside the likes of Terry, Gallas and Carvalho, the 20 year-old will aim to add more appearances for the first team this season.

The Wright Stuff

England winger Shaun Wright-Phillips became a Chelsea player in July 2005 after Manchester City reluctantly accepted a bid of £21million for the talented 23-year-old.

Darling of the City fans and a hero to thousands of youngsters, Shaun Wright-Phillips is one of the best players City have ever produced through the ranks. The dashing wide right star was at his best for much of the 2004/5 season and finally won his first England cap and scored on his debut against the Ukraine. But his career began far less spectacularly and, hard though it may seem to believe, Shaun could easily have ended up on the soccer scrap heap aged 16 when he was released by Nottingham Forest who felt he was too small to succeed in top-level football.

Along with his younger brother Bradley, he travelled to Manchester where City took him on and he soon made a big impression on the coaches at the club's Academy. A couple of years later he made his first team debut away to Burnley and from that moment on, life was never the same again for the adopted son of former Arsenal legend Ian Wright. His all-action, whole-hearted performances soon made him a huge crowd favourite and when Kevin Keegan became manager in 2001, he said that Shaun would one day become an England regular.

Voted Young Player of the Year for three years in succession, the youngster was soon a regular in City's first team and wearing the No.29 shirt, he became a vital member of City's team for four seasons and in September 2004, after being voted City's Player of the Year for 2003/04, he finally won his first full England cap. He came on as a second half substitute and within minutes scored with a trademark dribble and low drive against Ukraine.

The spotlight was now firmly on the London-born right midfielder and he continued to excel for his club Manchester City. His sizzling club form saw him earn more England caps last season as well as notching up 10 spectacular goals. He also played a big part in City's 1-0 win over the Blues last season – but we'll forgive him for that!

Despite signing a new four-year deal at the start of last season, speculation linking him with a move to Stamford Bridge continued all summer and in early July, the Blues officially lodged a bid of £20m for the player. City, feeling the depth of their fans' concerns over losing the crowd idol, rejected the offer but despite originally saying he wanted to stay in Manchester, the lure of Champions League football and the chance of winning medals and a place in the England 2006 World Cup squad proved too strong and when the Blues upped their bid £1m, City – reluctantly – accepted.

Shaun Wright-Phillips is without doubt one of the most exciting prospects in English football and he will soon be wooing a whole new set of fans with his dynamic play – but this time at Stamford Bridge, wearing a darker shade blue!

Asier del Horno

Spanish international defender Asier del Horno signed for the Blues during the summer for a fee of around £8m from Athletic Bilbao. The left-back spot proved troublesome after Wayne Bridge's injury last season with central defender William Gallas covering the position. The 24 year-old will now compete with Bridge for a regular spot in the starting eleven.

2004/05 Season Quiz

1. James Beattie
2. Bolton
3. Porto
4. Crystal Palace
5. False – It was 96,650 v Barcelona
6. Manchester City
7. Newcastle United
8. Jiri Jarosik
9. Joe Cole v Birmingham
10. 11 – Leon McKenzie of Norwich

Name Game Quiz

1. Carlo Cudicini
2. Arjen Robben
3. Didier Drogba
4. William Gallas
5. Claude Makelele
6. Ricardo Carvalho
7. Damien Duff
8. Robert Huth
9. Frank Lampard
10. Tiago

Who Are They?

1. Arjen Robben
2. William Gallas
3. Peter Cech
4. Frank Lampard
5. Joe Cole
6. John Terry

Spot the Ball

Spot the Differences

Wordsearch

Crossword